Songs of My Soul

To Paul,

How beautiful on the mountains are the
feet of the messenger who brings good
news, the good news of peace
and salvation, the news
that the God of Israel reigns!
-Isaiah 52:7 (NLT)

Love and Peace,

Ray

Songs of My Soul

Poems, Prayers, and Meditations

Raymond Mulligan

WESTBOW
PRESS®
A DIVISION OF THOMAS NELSON
& ZONDERVAN

Copyright © 2018 Raymond Mulligan.

All rights reserved. No part of this book may be used or reproduced by any means, graphic, electronic, or mechanical, including photocopying, recording, taping or by any information storage retrieval system without the written permission of the author except in the case of brief quotations embodied in critical articles and reviews.

This book is a work of non-fiction. Unless otherwise noted, the author and the publisher make no explicit guarantees as to the accuracy of the information contained in this book and in some cases, names of people and places have been altered to protect their privacy.

Cover photograph by Raymond Mulligan
Pleasant River Sunrise, Addison, Maine

"Scripture quotations are from the ESV® Bible (The Holy Bible, English Standard Version®), copyright © 2001 by Crossway, a publishing ministry of Good News Publishers. Used by permission. All rights reserved."

Scripture taken from the New King James Version®. Copyright © 1982 by Thomas Nelson. Used by permission. All rights reserved.

THE HOLY BIBLE, NEW INTERNATIONAL VERSION®, NIV® Copyright © 1973, 1978, 1984, 2011 by Biblica, Inc.® Used by permission. All rights reserved worldwide.

Scripture quotations marked (NLT) are taken from the Holy Bible, New Living Translation, copyright © 1996, 2004, 2007 by Tyndale House Foundation. Used by permission of Tyndale House Publishers, Inc., Carol Stream, Illinois 60188. All rights reserved.

WestBow Press books may be ordered through booksellers or by contacting:

WestBow Press
A Division of Thomas Nelson & Zondervan
1663 Liberty Drive
Bloomington, IN 47403
www.westbowpress.com
1 (866) 928-1240

Because of the dynamic nature of the Internet, any web addresses or links contained in this book may have changed since publication and may no longer be valid. The views expressed in this work are solely those of the author and do not necessarily reflect the views of the publisher, and the publisher hereby disclaims any responsibility for them.

Any people depicted in stock imagery provided by Getty Images are models, and such images are being used for illustrative purposes only. Certain stock imagery © Getty Images.

ISBN: 978-1-9736-3880-3 (sc)
ISBN: 978-1-9736-3882-7 (hc)
ISBN: 978-1-9736-3881-0 (e)

Library of Congress Control Number: 2018910567

Print information available on the last page.

WestBow Press rev. date: 09/18/2018

I will sing to the LORD as long as I live;
I will sing praise to my God while I have being.
—Psalm 104:33 (ESV)

Praise for *Songs of My Soul*

The relentless tenderness of Ray Mulligan's poems touches the heartstrings, creating gentle melodies. Their simplicity evokes the depth from which they spring. The questions they raise arise from faith and lead to faith. The clear, pure notes they sound refresh one's spirit. They welcome you to their blessings.

—Phil Johnson, editor emeritus, *Pietisten*

My poetry is dedicated to the many poets and poetic writers, past and present, famous and not-so-famous who write from their souls and in turn stir my soul. I am very thankful for the time that I have been able to spend reading and contemplating their works. The following list identifies some of these poets, presented in no particular order:

The Book of Psalms
Thomas Merton
Maya Angelou
Rainer Maria Rilke
Robina Sloan
Laura Mazza-Dixon
Mattie Stepanek
Tom Mazzeo
Robert Bly
Ann Voskamp
William Wordsworth
William Butler Yeats
Walt Whitman
Basho
Henry David Thoreau
St. John of the Cross

Acknowledgments

In the same way that no man is an island, no book is published without many helping hands. Sometimes the helping hands are miles away, and at other times they are just a smile away, or even present in the Holy Spirit. The following represent those helping hands who have assisted me in completing my book of poetry.

Phillip D. Johnson—Phil is a longtime friend, published author, and editor emeritus of an ecumenical journal. He eagerly agreed to be the first reader of my manuscript.

Doris Barton—Doris is a lovely lady and longtime, dear friend who very graciously agreed to be one of my readers. She is a former teacher and volunteer worker.

Lorna Ross-Purvin—Lorna is a recently made friend who teaches sacred dance. She enthusiastically agreed to be one of my readers.

Thursday Morning Faith Group—This is a seniors group that I lead twice a month from our church family in Connecticut. They have been continuously supportive during this project; they are my cheerleaders.

Our campground friends in Maine, where we spend our summers, have been very supportive and encouraging during our summer months there.

The Holy Spirit—This entire project has been Spirit-led and Spirit-guided. Thank you, Lord.

My wife, Sally, who has been in my corner for fifty-six years. Thank you, Sal. Thanks for your patience.

The folks at WestBow Press—all the people that I have had contact with have been extremely cordial, courteous, and helpful. Thank you.

Contents

Introduction xix

Prelude 1

Abandoned 3

Holy Hymns 5

My Lord of Peace 7

Evict the Darkness 8

Summer Respite 9

He Calls Me 10

Strengthened by Your Love 11

This Is My Beloved 12

Temptation 13

Broadway 14

Lake of Light 15

Your Child 16

Saint Patrick's Legacy 17

The Evil One's Lair 18

Mystical Thoughts 19

The Face 20

Our Passion 21

Some Moments along My Way 23

The Children's Home 25

Affirmation 26

But Going Where? 27

Brothers in Christ 29

Craig's Flowers 30

My Walden 31

Autumn Leaves 32

The Checkout Line 33

What Are You Doing? 34

Humble Healing Hands 35

Lifeless Without You 36

This God-sent Child 37

Grandsons 38

Little Moments 39

Abruptly 40

Born Again 41

God's Intention 42

Meeting Vincent 43

Softly 45

Joy 46

Uncle Jimmy 47

Fortieth Reunion 48

Desertion 49

Profane Pebbles 51

The Prince 53

Whitman Songs 54

Whitman's Legacy 55

Amid His Tears 56

Discouraged 57

Loneliness 58

Intimacy 59

Through the Eyes of Our Hearts 60

Paradise 61

Shimmering Hearts 62

Divine Splendor 63

Reflection 64

Wondering, Pondering 65

Gray Stones 66

Sacred Stories 67

My Brother of the Brambles 68

The Sacred Pond 70

Christ for Me 73

Freedom 75

An Awesome Place 77

My Hungarian Rhapsody 79

Prayers 81

My Prayer to Our Father 83

Praying My Discomfort 84

Two Prayers 85

Meditations 87

Your Way 89

Amazing God 90

Heavenly Hills 91

Glory Light 92

Guideposts 93

Still There? 94

True Hope 95

Thinking of Me? Wow! 96

From My Heart 97

Send Me 98

Beware 99

Our Condition 100

Eternal Flame 101

God's Presence 102

Who May Enter 103

Rain on Me 104

Seek You, First 105

Your Lamp of Love 106

Starry Night 107

My Heart's Desire 108

Anything More? 109

Trust 110

My Soul Is Empty, Lord 111

Postlude 113

Abba, Father 115

Epilogue 117

Grateful Praise, Hallelujah 119

References and Source Acknowledgments 123

About the Author 125

Introduction

Our souls are the treasury of our heart-felt experiences that connect us with our eternal God; "He has planted eternity in the human heart" (Ecclesiastes 3:11 NIV). All of my poems, prayers, and meditations are spoken from my soul and should be read slowly and pondered one by one. Although the words of each poem provide the literal understanding, it is the deep-felt, *soulful* level of meaning that provides the divine truth. The poems represent a collection of some of my soul-filled experiences during these many years of my journey. Each poem is a gift from the fullness of God's creation. My hope is that you will find God's beauty in each of them. So savor, enjoy, and be surprised with each gift.

We are not human beings having a spiritual experience.
We are spiritual beings having a human experience.
    —Pierre Teilhard de Chardin

Prelude

You will forget your misery; it will
be like water flowing away.
—Job 11:16 (NLT)

Abandoned

The storm,
raging from deep within
with groans and growls of disgust,
banging on the flood gates in anger,
encompassing a lifetime.

Swearing surges, in-bursting
to restrain out-bursting,
were half century gathered
but contained and unrevealed,
the father's sin still shrieking in memory.

The lovers,
casting out the mother,
their flesh and desire enthroned,
now the basis of their deceit;
their deception then delivered … done.

Three little lives
interrupted from flow,
innocent victims betrayed;
motherless, fatherless …
abandoned!

"Where is love?"
the little one cries.
Silence brings the answer;
the Life Father watches,
waiting to answer, waiting to answer …

Holy Hymns

O God, you are my God; earnestly I seek you; my soul thirsts for you; my flesh faints for you, as in a dry and weary land where there is no water.
—Psalm 63:1 (ESV)

My Lord of Peace

Wait patiently for the LORD. Be brave and courageous.
Yes, wait patiently for the LORD.
—Psalm 27:14 (NLT)

Sanctuary …
the garden,
alone with my Spirit,
all absence of din,
ego and vanity stripped at the gate.

Quietude greets this sojourner,
manna to my soul;
silence my preparation,
anticipating His voice,
His presence … my Lord.

Jehovah Shalom,
my Lord of peace.
My spirit from His essence,
my life through Him,
my death in Him.

For Him I wait …
my Lord of peace,
Jehovah Shalom.

Evict the Darkness

The LORD is my light and my salvation.
—Psalm 27:1a (NLT)

The evil one lurks in my darkness,
lying in wait for my life,
tempting my weaknesses,
probing my vulnerabilities;
my heaviness belongs to him.

The Holy One's light is constant,
bright, and eternally shining,
ever beckoning,
ever welcoming;
fling wide the doors of salvation,
evict the darkness with light!

Hallelujah!

Summer Respite

He leads me beside quiet waters, he refreshes my soul.
—Psalm 23:2b (NIV)

Somehow, a few moments,
a gift, a pause from dailiness,
an escape of the heart, of the mind contained,
transcending toil.

Feet wandering along, comfortably,
mind fogged in the clouds,
heart flying the breeze
to the pond's edge.

It is so natural to be drawn
to these waters of love,
where life is sacred and true,
and joyfully swim to God's glorious delight.

Soothing and healing this refreshment of soul,
my respite nearly complete;
by Son and salvation, the granting of peace,
my soul reaffirmed and fed.

He Calls Me

Come to me, all you who are weary and
burdened, and I will give you rest.
—Matthew 11:28 (NIV)

In beauty He calls me,
fraught from the weariness of life.
His radiance fills my soul,
His voice quickens my heart.
My Lord bids me, "Come."

Strengthened by Your Love

Therefore put on the full armor of God,
so that when the day of evil comes, you
may be able to stand your ground.
—Ephesians 6:13 (NIV)

Again I go out to mingle with the world …
staving off barbs, feeling the sting of arrows,
but still, I hold fast to Your truth.

Then I am strengthened by Your love and
saved by "the sword of the Spirit"—
Your Word.

The sword of the Spirit.
—Ephesians 6:17 (NIV)

This Is My Beloved

As the Father has loved me, so have I loved you.
—John 15:9 (NIV)

This is my beloved, my dear ...
my fullness,
my weakness,
my passion,
unknowing my fear!

This is my beloved, my desire ...
fairest to me,
opening to me,
mingling with me,
consuming ecstasy, my fire!

This is my beloved,
my Lord!

Temptation

So, if you think you are standing firm,
be careful that you don't fall!
—1 Corinthians 10:12 (NIV)

Temptation,
ever before me,
remnant of evil's banishment,
reminder of unworthiness,
of Adam's struggle.
Temptation,
a constant presence.

Broadway

The highway to hell is broad, and its gate is
wide ... But the gateway to life is very narrow.
—Matthew 7:13–14 (NLT)

Broadway—
perverted truth!
Bright flashing lights
diverting the traveler,
bypassing the narrow way.
How much farther to Babylon?
How much farther to sin and death?

Lake of Light

For you were once darkness, but now you are
light in the LORD. Live as children of light.
—Ephesians 5:8 (NIV)

For what child,
in the virtue of his youth,
living in the wildness
and beauty of nature,
would not bathe in the lake of light?

For that child,
alive as a son of creation,
is the holy child of God,
joyfully immersed in the warmth of the lake,
gleefully splashing in the light of our Lord.

Your Child

And he took the children in his arms.
—Mark 10:16 (NIV)

In my sophomoric youth,
I ran from this,
frightened by Your touch,
denying my deep feelings,
fearful of succumbing to Your love.

But as a child,
I leaped into Your arms,
eagerly kissing You,
hugging You with all my might,
joyously aglow in Your affection.

And now, grasping the folly of my youth,
weary from loneliness,
burdened by life's meaninglessness,
I hurry to You with unerring desire
to again be Your child.

Saint Patrick's Legacy

I arise today through the strength of Heaven.
—Saint Patrick, "The Deer's Cry"

I rise this day
afresh in the dew of my creation,
bathed in the light of God,
clothed in the love of Christ,
and rejoicing in the dawning of my spirit.

I rise this day
professing the omnipotence of the Trinity,
the eternity of oneness,
the promise of salvation,
and proclaiming the mystery of the cross.

I rise this day
by the grace of God,
accepting Christ's challenge to fullness,
seeking Christ's presence in life's dailiness,
and living the love of Jesus.

I rise this day
to the glory of God!

The Evil One's Lair

Your enemy, the devil, prowls around like a
roaring lion looking for someone to devour.
—1 Peter 5:8 (NIV)

Holding out, alone,
tiring, wearing,
sometimes stumbling, falling …
laid bare in the evil one's lair.

Here, my weaknesses fully exposed,
stroked by the devil's torment,
thrust boldly before me;
he, lustfully laughing, blasphemously sneering,

*Ah, my dearest, my delight,
my succulent sweet,
how lovely thy nakedness …
your ripeness, my feast!*

Sing to me, my Redeemer,
ring truth as my bell,
shine light along the right path,
and lead me away from this tempter.

Sin is not in my heart!

Mystical Thoughts

Such knowledge is too wonderful for me,
too lofty for me to attain.
—Psalm 139:6 (NIV)

Mystical thoughts
on celestial mind-ways,
connecting eternity,
confounding my logic,
amusing their Creator.

The Face

My heart says of you, "Seek his face!"
Your face, Lord, I will seek.
—Psalm 27:8 (NIV)

The face,
the glorious face,
the glorious face of love.
His face …
your face,
my friend!

Our Passion

Unfailing love and truth have met together.
Righteousness and peace have kissed!
—Psalm 85:10 (NLT)

My life,
my mystery,
my love,
my passion.

His life,
His mystery,
His love,
His passion.

Our Lord,
our light,
our love,
our passion!

Some Moments along My Way

Trust in the L<small>ORD</small> with all your heart,
and lean not on your own understanding;
in all your ways acknowledge Him,
and He shall direct your paths.
—Proverbs 3:5–6 (NKJV)

The Children's Home

There you sit,
you lovely sonny boy,
so beautiful your smile,
so lively and bedeviled your ways.

But oh, you reluctant angel,
how indifferent you are to love;
how was God's grace
driven from you?

Look how you
clothe yourself in armor
with prankish ways
and peppery words.

Love you fend off,
too painful to embrace,
your heart still
suffering its wounds.

But one day, one moment,
you wary little one,
you will feel God's kiss;
you will know God's love.

And you will be freed in love!

Affirmation

Unexpected, startling—
like a static discharge—
yet always looked for,
always hoped for ...
these moments of
affirmation.

Being sensitized, attuned
to subtle treasures ...
of faces, of words,
free form, rhyming,
hearing the heart,
singing the soul, soaring the spirit.

Love's pretty face,
love's heartfelt smile,
love's dimple,
love's eyes ... meeting,
acknowledging feeling,
warmly shining.

Transitory but captured,
fixed in memory,
to bathe in, to play in,
to cuddle in ...
to know my Creator in!

But Going Where?

Those cold, steel bars
I had to reach through
to clasp your hand ...
your grip on my soul
shivered me.

I felt helpless
before your lifeless
form, thrown away
by life's crassness,
thrown back to die.

The years, space between us,
disconnected
but yet connected
by love's connectiveness,
disregarding time.

Again, being reminded to leave.
"Not family," said nursie,
not knowing we married
our souls years before;
you and I, love's family.

Our embracing smiles
soul-felt ...
the best that we could do;
those imprisoning side rails
and protective restraints ... Ha!

We talked foolishness
to spare our hearts;
we knew where we weren't
because of where we were,
you the suicidal one.

You the crazy,
me the sane,
bars apart,
lives apart.
We were once the same!

"You must go," saith nursie,
her curt rejection of my presence,
each of us being forced to leave—
but going where?
I think you knew better than I.

Brothers in Christ

I cannot tell you
who I am
or why our hearts
long as one …
only
that we seek
the same embrace, and
we are brothers.

Craig's Flowers

There,
beside the pasture fence;
there,
where you seeded them unpurposefully;
there,
where we discovered love's bond;
there,
where our hearts grew visibly ...

Your springtime resurrection!

My Walden

I have my Walden,
my precious solitude beside the pond
where my heart is moved,
and where my spirit attains flight ...
deep within my wounded soul,
your love.

Autumn Leaves

Leaves in flight
with colors bright,
falling beauty in my sight;
soft their sound,
they flutter down,
brilliant carpet on the ground.

Grace,
this splendor from above,
bathes our souls
in peaceful love.

The Checkout Line

The meeting of eyes,
the fleetest of moments.
I, focused on mission, turning away,
no allowances for distraction.
"Ahem" proclaiming your presence,
my cause for attention,
full turning provoked,
and capturing me.

Virtuous beauty!
Innocent spirit!
Pure light!
Precious little one!

Your smiling face,
Your radiant presence,
Your spontaneous gift of love
cuddling my heart.

What Are You Doing?

It is not enough to be busy. So are the ants.
The question is: What are we busy about?
—Henry David Thoreau

Never mind being pious
or praying
or reading the Bible ...
Never mind going to church
every Sunday
or singing in the choir ...
But, what are you doing?

What are *you* doing,
doing to love
and live like Jesus ...
going out beyond
your selfish self,
extending your heart and hand ...
What are you doing?

What am I doing?

Humble Healing Hands

The bath,
toil's awaited repose ...
disciples'
humble healing hands,
refreshing souls.

Lifeless Without You

How quickly I plummet
to darkness, to despair
in the absence of Your breath,
my spirit lifeless
without You.

This God-sent Child

Beautifully comes
the cherubic child,
dreaming in mystical fancies,
creating love's dances.

Freely gives
his virtuous gifts, lovely and lusty,
tender delights, bounding joys,
and naked innocence.

Sweetly slumbers
in blissful scapes,
gayful glades, sensuous seas,
warm sun and breeze, his chastely mates.

Ah, this Christly sprite,
pure and bright,
heart swelling, soul filling,
wounding light!

Merciful grace, this God-sent child.

Grandsons

To be kissed by a child is to be kissed by God.
—Author Unknown

Little eyes
greeting mine,
little smiles
meeting mine,
little hands
taking mine,
little lips
kissing mine,
little hearts
wounding mine ...

God's sweet angels of love.

Little Moments

Life is flat
in the absence of little ones

whose little laughs
and little giggles,
joyfully tickle ...

whose little smiles
and little kisses,
freely love ...

whose little hands
and little arms,
warmly hold ...

whose little hearts
and little souls,
wholly rest with mine

as little moments of knowing God.

Abruptly

I am certain of nothing but the holiness of the Heart's
affections and the truth of the Imagination.
—John Keats

Abruptly,
my whole being is startled
by your hand placed unexpectedly in mine,
your sudden closeness
overwhelming my heart.
You, tightly wrapping my arms about you
and resting content in the warmth of love.

And is that how it will be for me
at the moment of my birth,
boldly leaping into Your arms,
peering into Your eyes,
and glimpsing the glory
of my true being?

Born Again

If I can get beyond
these temporal constraints
and wholly experience
the fullness of my spirit,
I will know the Lord,
I will know, rebirth!

God's Intention

For no reason,
save love alone,
I live …
to love You!
To know Your beauty,
Your fullness;
to behold the Spirit of You,
and embrace …
You!

Meeting Vincent

Yes,
I see
that your skin
is a different color
than mine ...

But
what I see
more clearly is
our hearts
joyfully entwined.

Bliss

This feeling,
unknown before this moment,
uniquely created,
lovingly,
by You.

Softly

Softly,
His voice,
quiet assurances of presence,
purest whispers
of love.

Joy

This joy I feel
from being with you,
uplifting, intoxicating, warm;
delighting our hearts, uniting our souls,
in fellowship with our Lord.

Uncle Jimmy

Everybody loved Jimmy—
all the aunts and uncles,
brothers and sisters,
nieces and nephews.
They all called him Jay.
Beth hated that.

Everybody loved Jimmy.
I admired that,
wondering how that happened.
What was special about him?
Even people on the street
smiled and waved and called out,
"Hi, Jimmy!"

Everybody loved Jimmy.
That really bothered Beth,
that other people loved this man
perhaps as she couldn't;
their marriage flat and lifeless,
their lives without flavor or fruit.

Everybody loved Jimmy ...
including me!

Fortieth Reunion

Did you really think there wasn't anyone here
thinking of you?
—Grace

How wonderfully warming to know
our separation was felt;
a small soul not vanishing,
unnoticed …
that I was remembered,
so dearly!

And dare not think
our youthful treasure was lost—
our delightful dances,
our fondness of hearts.
Our friendship,
dear sister,
still prized!

Desertion

> Though my father and mother forsake me,
> the Lord will receive me.
> —Psalm 27:10 (NIV)

And when I die,
I shall cry
for all the love that I did not give,
that I could not give,
because of your betrayal.

Your love taunted me
but lessened the pain
that my soul contained,
for your hands that I could not hold
and my heart that hid, maimed.

Profane Pebbles

There is a time for everything, and a season
for every activity under the heavens.
—Ecclesiastes 3:1 (NIV)

The Prince

Beneath this cloak so old, so bare,
lives Nature's boy, so bold and fair.

With hair of red and freckled cheeks,
he sallies forth in quest of beasts!

Beclothed in grandeur, his suit from birth,
beware his merrymaking, full of mirth.

The Prince he's called by imp and sprite,
bedevilment and smiles his cunning might.

His giggle and laughter, his natural care,
his songs of love float freely to air.

This Prince, this tale, his story retold
keeps lively these bones beneath cloak so old.

Whitman Songs

Oh, to sing in harmony
the Whitman songs of comrades,
those strong, bold, lusty tunes
bequeathed to us
as boys, as youths, as men.
Arm in arm together in common bond,
honoring our inheritance with respect,
with reverence, with humility,
speaking openly,
living trustingly,
laughing boisterously,
united as brothers and praying as one,
as loving sons of creation.

Whitman's Legacy

Take these words, do with them as you wish.
Laugh with them,
love with them,
cry with them,
despair with them,
disgust with them,
glory in them.
They're not mine—
they're yours!

Amid His Tears

The boy, in the bloom of his youth,
in the flow of his years,
into the flow of the sea,
cast his wish for age
amid his tears.

The man, in the seed of his age,
in the ebb of his years,
into the ebb of the sea,
cast his wish for youth
amid his tears.

Discouraged

I despise this frustration,
this stagnation of thought,
total loss of clarity, discouraged;
feeling encumbered in my journey,
not involving myself in life,
not really living,
just going through the motions
of loving Him!

Loneliness

Loneliness expresses the pain of being alone
and solitude expresses the glory of being alone.
—Paul Tillich

Loneliness
sweeps over me like silent fog,
graying my senses,
imprisoning me in anxious mist.

Persistently it lingers
with penetrating wetness,
soaking me through,
chilling me to the bone.

Shivering, I flounder,
no longer certain of my course,
fears flogging me,
crippling my very will.

And so I flee,
seeking a safe harbor,
some sheltered refuge of quiet waters,
there to lay up in the sanctuary of my soul.

Ah, sweet solitude …
alone with my Lord.

Intimacy

Enter my mind,
fathom depth …

Enter my heart,
experience beauty …

Enter my body,
explore flesh …

Enter my soul,
discover truth …

Join with my spirit,
seek freedom …

Find me,
find yourself!

Through the Eyes of Our Hearts

Come, my beloved,
and journey with me awhile
to places before unknown to us,
creations of Spirit and intimacy.

Come, my beloved,
carefully down these frightful cliffs
to caverns deep and dank,
exploring the murmurings of our hearts.

Come, my beloved,
to the hidden place of quiet waters,
to refresh our thirsty souls,
drinking the flowing spring eternal.

Come, my beloved,
slowly, gently, lifting our veils,
to reveal our innocence and beauty,
bathed in the light that never darkens.

Come, my beloved,
stand close to embrace our love,
to warm the flesh of our lives,
bonding in the passion of oneness.

Come, my beloved …

Paradise

Somewhere,
my beloved,
out beyond these temporal trappings
is Paradise,
There we will meet.

And there we will love
completely,
as innocent virgins
in blissful passion,
two spirits consummating oneness.

Shimmering Hearts

Our shimmering hearts,
ripplings of moonlight on the pond,
sparkling reflections on timorous bathers,
tenderly revealing
love's adornment.

Divine Splendor

If you think of me
as your beloved, I am;
and if you wonder
about our closeness, so do I.

For I am your beloved,
as you are mine;
our eyes, in greeting,
reveal their warmth and treasure.

Adventurously,
let us leap across the stars,
swim in ancient pools,
lie on pristine shores,
our hearts delighting in passion.

Quietly,
let us hold to each,
exploring Nature's bond,
discovering our depths,
our souls resounding in truth.

So join with me
and dare to know
the beauty of our love;
even friendship
will be divine!

Reflection

Always moving,
man's always pushing on ...
pushing out from himself,
rarely from inward focus,
and always further from center.
For what?

I detest the responsive credo,
"For progress!"
Progress toward what? What's the goal
of this mania and madness,
of this incessant drive,
of not being caught motionless?

And the hurry of it all—
depersonalizing, distancing,
leaving so little left to get close to,
so little left that invites knowing.
And the hurry of it all.
For what?

So I am resisting,
purposefully steering away
from mindless mainstream thought,
seeking the vantage point,
reflection, and challenging ...
Progress for what? For God?
Whose God?

Wondering, Pondering

So many things to think about,
so many things to wonder:
trees, leaves,
grass, flowers,
crickets, frogs,
sunshine, rain, stars …
So many things!

So many things to think about,
so many things to ponder:
parents, children,
brothers, sisters,
friends, lovers,
laughter, tears, broken hearts …
So many things!

And evil …?

Gray Stones

Gray stones,
chiseled shapes,
blocks, columns, piled high mausoleums,
stories of lives remembered.

Gray stones,
temporal tombs,
stoic monuments to dust,
silent sentinels of death.

Gray stones,
warmly bathed in morning light,
cold silhouettes on moonlit night …
marking flight!

Sacred Stories

And God said, "Let there be lights in the vault of the sky to separate the day from the night, and let them serve as signs to mark sacred times, and days and years …" And it was so.
—Genesis 1:14–15 (NIV)

My Brother of the Brambles

He reached down from on high and took hold of me.
—2 Samuel 22:17a (NIV)

Going out into the magic of the morning,
anticipating the pleasures of the venture,
our senses fully flushed,
piqued for the hunt for life's luscious fruits,
the plumpest of the berries ... what a quest!

Off to our private patch we clamored
to pick our pails full to flowing,
and then to eat, and pick some more,
always daring, always seeking the best berries,
risking ourselves in lustful challenge,
inching farther into the brambles,
toward the darkened den and ... falling!

Looking up through the brambles,
the sun's brilliance streaming through,
such stunning light,
marking clear the thorns in silhouette,
still glistening my blood on their tips.

Life's passages, festooned
with Lucifer fruit and brambles,
ensnaring the unwary,
piercing their beauty, their virtue,
leaving scaring stripes painted on their passions
of living and loving and helpless will.

Now, my brother, how radiant this Son,
sacrificing Himself to the brambles,
reaches down into my dark prison
seeking my hand, mercifully touching
my marred nature with penetrating warmth,
lifts me, frees me,
and leads me out into the fullness of light
and healing wholeness.

The Sacred Pond

> Remember your Creator in the days of your youth,
> before the days of trouble come.
> —Ecclesiastes 12:1 (NIV)

I meander through these now solitary woods
fondly refreshing each living moment,
pausing by the pond,
catching glimpses of a joyous past:
vaporous vignettes of boisterous boys
consumed in natural abandon,
unconcerned with worldly clamor,
steeped only in childhood's god
and friendships long and lasting.

In captive sunlit hours
filled with laughter
and shouts of challenging bucks,
our swimming hole madness
created our camaraderie,
flashing flurries of brutishness,
balanced by brotherly intimacies,
growing in the spirit of Sonship,
nurtured by the grace of our Creator.

We swam in blissful nakedness,
this brotherhood of innocent sprites,
splashed with revelry and delight,
till lips turned blue and
our goose-bumped bodies
shivered for warmth.

Then, and only then, reluctantly,
like cold, lethargic reptiles,
we dragged ourselves onto the sunning rocks
for warmth, for rest ... for soul.

There was where we lived and dreamed
and basked in our sensual selves,
celebrating our blossoming boyhood,
exploring our mythical enchantments,
indifferent to our approaching destiny,
manhood,
and the unrealized sacrifice of our
virtuous youth.

Persistently we pushed that off,
that manhood stuff,
not willing to relinquish
our Edenic sanctuary,
joyfully lingering
beyond boyhood
to escape those tormenting times
of frightful adolescence.

Sometimes we sunned in silence,
in brilliant glory,
in appreciation of ourselves,
of each other,
of God's endowment
of our being,
the unspoken revelations of Spirit and self ...

Often we embroiled
the quiet water,
leaping, shouting, singing
the songs of sons,
or lounged in our sun-fast moments of beauty,
oblivious to our future darkness,
of days without each other …
future eternities of separation.

But then, we didn't care, we didn't know,
for those moments were of us and in us, in
our bodies,
our hearts,
our souls;
in living and being boys;
in being free …
free from sin, free in love,
free in brotherhood,
free in our Creator …
fully free in the Spirit
as sons.

This poem is dedicated to my brother Donald
who passed away, Sunday, August 19, 2018.

Christ for Me

> Christ within me, Christ beside me.
> —Saint Patrick, "The Deer's Cry"

There was love about You,
Your smile, Your essence,
a remnant of innocence,
but innocent not,
neither You nor I.

Even then You knew me,
as I did not,
my mask ever convincing to me;
Your warmth, an aura all-inviting,
a mystery, unspoken but seen.

Abruptly convergent our paths,
You standing alongside mine,
and I saw You that day
as goodness and light;
the one of eternity I seek.

How utterly foolish this thought!
How completely left-brained!
Your resurrection, even then, not believed;
but here before me, arisen as light,
shining brightly and free ... Christ for me!

But my reality returned,
my disparities of perception,
my barriers to faith and belief;
timidity loud, misgivings rampant,
my Redeemer seemed approachless by me.

Have faith, dear friend.
Take courage, my brother.
Your heart is aching His love;
this Son of Creation is given to you!
This day, this life, this eternity.

So, with stumbling heart and mumbling mind,
I accepted Your call of love,
and now our friendship and fellowship,
with Christ as our center,
entwines our souls eternally.

Freedom

No love, no friendship, can cross the path of our
destiny without leaving some mark on it forever.
—Francois Mauriac

You came to me,
an impetuous youth, full of life, full of love,
How quickly you befriended me.

You were the wood sprite,
a spirit of joy,
delivering your gift to me.
How was I the moment of your treasure?

Many a day we were companions,
with nature, with laughter, with bedevilment;
the wisdom you revealed for life,
the eventual dread of your sadness, and mine.

Our closeness, not lengthy,
too quickly left us,
our journey no longer together.
We each went onward, stoically onward,
realizing this curse of an end.

It was one day and then another,
your fate unfolding.
How could this be?
Your rainbow collapsing,
my friend.

Now, torment is over, your suffering gone.
Our Savior awaits you, so go.
His arms enfold you,
soaring you homeward.
Freedom at last with our Lord.

And I miss you, dear brother,
sweet son of the Father.
This heart is behind you, my friend,
but the promise for tomorrow is given today,
with reunion eternal …

Amen.

An Awesome Place

> How awesome is this place! This is none other than
> the house of God; this is the gate of heaven.
> —Genesis 28:17 (NIV)

Sitting on these rocks high above the river,
resting between earth and sky,
the calm of the river below, quieting the
echoes of conscious clamor,
creating moments for contemplation,
on being human ... on living in the mystery.

Bathed now in God's glorious warmth,
wrapped in His early autumn tapestry,
and accompanied by Nature's choir
still heard above fragrant earthy breezes—
busy creatures singing out their given songs—
I listen for the sound of His voice,
its beauty filling my soul.

Long my lonely soul has searched,
seeking the holy way to abiding love,
the joyful beginning of true communion,
of absolute love,
there to rest and feast
at the banquet of love's union.

Now I glimpse love's glory,
the innocent child going forth
in the virtue and beauty of his Lord,
only his wistful cries and songs
guiding him to the open arms
of love, there to be held
in the fullness of his Father's heart.

How amazing this place,
Love's sweetest repose,
no crippling fears of loneliness,
of impoverishment,
only God's face-to-face love
and its recreating wholeness.
Here, in this awesome place, my soul finds rest!

Blessed Shalom.

Peace is the beauty of life. It is sunshine. It is the smile of a child, the love of a mother, the joy of a father, the togetherness of a family. It is the advancement of man, the victory of a just cause, the triumph of truth.
—Menachem Begin

My Hungarian Rhapsody

I was a stranger, and you invited me into your home.
—Matthew 25:35 (NLT)

Oh, Hungary,
how strong your hold on me.
You welcome me as your brother,
greeting me with kindness and love.

Lustily I bathe in your charm,
captivated by your enchantment,
the many manifestations
of a thousand years of richness.

Within you,
I joyously walk in the spirit,
embraced by your rapturous love,
discovering the bliss of my true self.

This affection,
so startling, so bewildering!
A nonsensical silliness to my mind,
not logical, totally impractical …
yet, still there.

And it is your beauty,
your unseen truth,
that pierces my heart
and wounds my inner sacredness.

I am in awe
of this wondrous mystery,
these soulful missions that draw me to you;
a mystery still unfolding.

So dare not end this
or I shall surely perish;
but lead me back to your bountiful love,
and our delightful reunion of souls.

Prayers

Rejoice always, pray continually.
—1 Thessalonians 5:16–17 (NIV)

My Prayer to Our Father

Hear, O LORD, and answer me, for I am poor and needy.
—Psalm 86:1 (NIV)

Lose to me, my Father,
Your tenderness. Let me
rest in the warmth of Your essence,
never leaving me to myself.

For there I am ... mist,
non-existent in Your absence,
only alive in Your presence.
Hold me to Your breast.

Father, hear my prayer.

Praying My Discomfort

You have shown me the way of life, and you
will fill me with the joy of your presence.
—Acts 2:28 (NLT)

Each day I struggle
with my humanness;
my ego,
my vanity,
my sensual self ...
my indifference to Your love.

O Lord,
let my discomfort
be Your calling
in the darkness,
coming to me,
choosing me,
leading me
out of this great night
and into the light of Your heart
and our joyous dance
of love.

Two Prayers

O Lord,
fill my mind with thoughts of You
and let my soul find rest;
keep me safe throughout my day,
and evening find me blessed.
Amen.

Merciful and loving Father,
let Your love
rain down like showers of blessings,
drenching me in Your mercy,
soaking me through to my soul.
May Your blessings never cease
and may they never fail,
as I may never cease and never fail
from loving You.
Hear my prayer, O Lord.
Amen.

Meditations

O God, we meditate on your unfailing
love as we worship in your temple.
—Psalm 48:9 NLT

Your Way

Blessed is the one who does not walk in step with
the wicked or stand in the way that sinners take.
—Psalm 1:1 (NIV)

O Lord,
each day I strive to make my way Your way.
Let Your Word guide my steps,
blessing me throughout my day.
In my prayers
I ask for Your forgiveness
and to walk in the light
of Your way.

Amazing God

Serve the LORD with fear and rejoice with trembling.
—Psalm 2:11 (ESV)

Amazing God!
You flood my imagination beyond words,
my joy bubbles up through me.
On my knees I worship You
and humbly serve
in your name.

Heavenly Hills

I call out to the LORD and he answers me
from his holy mountain.
—Psalm 3:4 (NIV)

I lift up my eyes
and open my heart
to You, O Lord,
and call out Your name in prayer.
From Your heavenly hills
You bless me
and call me to You,
there.

Glory Light

Let the light of your face shine on us.
Fill my heart with joy.
—Psalm 4:6b-7a (NIV)

Glory light
shining down from above;
warm, beautiful blessings.
My heart leaps for joy
as You fill my soul
with Your love.

Guideposts

Lead me in the right path, O LORD, or my enemies will conquer me. Make your way plain for me to follow.
—Psalm 5:8 (NLT)

Through the daily
hubbub and hullabaloo
lies Your way; it is well established.
I put on my Jesus glasses
to clearly see Your guideposts marked,
"The Way, the Truth, and the Life."

Still There?

My soul is in deep anguish. How
long, LORD, how long?
—Psalm 6:3 (NIV)

Like David, Lord,
my soul is in agony.
Evil and wickedness are everywhere;
children are being slaughtered!
Your silence breaks my heart.
Surely You are still there?

True Hope

O LORD my God, in you I put my trust.
—Psalm 7:1a (NIV)

Who else but You, Lord?
Our earthly princes and kings
have failed us completely.
Only in You is there true hope—
in You alone!

Thinking of Me? Wow!

What are mere mortals that you should think about
them, human beings that you should care for them?
—Psalm 8:4 (NLT)

Living souls,
like grains of sand on a beach
too numerous to count.
Yet You think of us, You care about us.
Now I understand the importance of Godly living;
I get it!
I can't disappoint
You.

From My Heart

I will praise you, LORD, with all my heart.
I will be filled with joy because of you.
—Psalm 9:1a–2a (NLT)

Hear me sing, Lord.
I'm so proud my buttons are popping.
Let the whole world hear my praise for You.
Let my song fill the heavens.
My song, Lord,
is from my heart.

Send Me

LORD, you know the hopes of the helpless. Surely
you will hear their cries and comfort them.
—Psalm 10:17 (NLT)

O Lord, send me!
Let me be a beacon in the midst of their darkness,
bringing Your light,
Your love,
filling their souls with
hope.

Beware

For behold, the wicked bend the bow; they
have fitted their arrow to the string to shoot
in the dark at the upright in heart.
—Psalm 11:2 (ESV)

The morning ritual for my daily commute;
putting on *the full armor of God*.
Every day, everywhere,
I fend off the slings and arrows,
deflecting the evil one's constant bombardment.
He never stops, he never tires.
Beware!

The full armor of God.
—Ephesians 6:13 (NIV)

Our Condition

Help, O LORD, for the godly are fast disappearing!
The faithful have vanished from the earth!
—Psalm 12:1 (NLT)

Our condition:
rampant indifference and constant hurry.
The need for speed has
overwhelmed the holiness of worship and prayer.
Who takes time to think about the vastness of God?
Who even considers the empty tomb?
Sadly, "whatever" is the new norm,
and hurry is our nemesis.

Eternal Flame

I will sing to the LORD because he is good to me.
—Psalm 13:6 (NLT)

Like an eternal flame, Lord,
Your light always shines.
Your love never stops warming my heart;
even my sinfulness does not dim
Your light.
I will always praise Your forgiveness
and Your goodness to me.

God's Presence

God is present in the company of the righteous.
—Psalm 14:5b (NIV)

Where does God abide?
Certainly not in the company of unbelievers,
those who say, "There is no God."
But here, with the faithful, the believers,
those who seek God,
and those who know the hope in the Resurrection,
God is with them.

Who May Enter

Who may worship in your sanctuary, LORD? Who may enter your presence on your holy hill?
—Psalm 15:1 (NLT)

Surely the righteous—
those who live out their daily lives
keeping My commandments
and seek My forgiveness for their sins,
and repent.

Also,
those who long to worship Me,
those who seek a better way,
all who desire to escape their darkness
and to live in My light—
invite them in,
yes!

Rain on Me

> I say to the LORD, You are my LORD;
> I have no good apart from you.
> —Psalm 16:2 (ESV)

Like a tree deprived of water,
I produce no fruit
without You, Lord.
You are my water,
my life-giving water.
So come water me, Lord,
rain on me,
soak me through to my roots.
Let me bear fruit
for Your glory.

Seek You, First

I am praying to you because I know you will
answer, O God. Bend down and listen as I pray.
—Psalm 17:6–7a (NLT)

Thank You, Lord, thank You.
You already know my mind and my heart,
You know my joys and my sadness,
and my life's regrets,
of which there is really only one:
that I have not loved You more.
Please forgive me, Lord.
It's only because of You
that I have come through the rain,
and now I see the rainbow.
In all my ways, Lord,
I will seek You
and love You,
first.

Your Lamp of Love

You light a lamp for me. The LORD,
my God, lights up my darkness.
—Psalm 18:28 (NLT)

In those night-filled days,
I thought You were
gone;
I felt lonely.
But then suddenly
in my darkness,
Your kiss,
Your light,
Your lamp of love
guiding me back
to You.
Oh, what joy!
Thank You, Lord.
Thank You for
Your unfailing love.

Starry Night

The heavens declare the glory of God; the
skies proclaim the work of his hands.
—Psalm 19:1 (NIV)

Just look up
at that *Starry Night* sky.
Astounding!
Amazing!
Awesome!
Impossible to comprehend or even fathom,
it renders our human logic useless.
Creation
our mystery,
but not Yours,
O Lord.

(Starry Night is a painting by Vincent van Gogh)

My Heart's Desire

May he grant your heart's desires and
make all your plans succeed.
—Psalm 20:4 (NLT)

O God,
You are my heart's desire!
May You always be at the top
of my list;
all else is secondary.
Let Your plans be my plans,
our plans,
with Your goodness and mercy
blessing me throughout my life.
Then, welcome me
into eternity
with You.

Anything More?

You have endowed him with eternal blessings
and given him the joy of your presence.
—Psalm 21:6 (NLT)

Who could ask for anything more, Lord?
You by my side
as my life's companion;
You as my guide,
leading me on the right path;
You as my light,
the beacon of my hope;
You as my eternal joy.
Is there really anything more?

Trust

In you our ancestors put their trust; they
trusted and you delivered them.
—Psalm 22:4 (NIV)

After faith and belief,
it's all about trust,
isn't it, Lord?
For many of us,
this is where we're at.
So here's the question:
"If You did that for our ancestors,
why wouldn't You do the same for us,
deliver us?"
Help our unbelief, Lord.

My Soul Is Empty, Lord

He restores my soul.
—Psalm 23:3a (NKJV)

My empty soul aches
for Your presence, Lord.
So lead me, my Shepherd Lord,
lead me to a quiet place,
a special place,
where it's just You and me—
a flowering field or a peaceful pond.
And let me rest in Your love
for a while.
Refresh me, Lord.
Come fill my soul with Your love.
Let my cup overflow.

Postlude

Oh, sing to the Lord a new song! ...Shout joyfully
to the LORD, all the earth.
—Psalm 98:1a, 4a (NKJV)

Abba, Father

Abba, Father,
to You, my song …
the song of Your giving,
of happiness,
of tears,
of love,
of joy …
of all that is me, of me, in me,
of Spirit,
of essence …
singing my soul
in harmonies
of innocence,
of beauty,
of truth …
singing boldly, sometimes timidly,
yet always my song
of my Creator,
to my Creator;
my song of
faith against unfaith,
of Your
faith against unfaith …
of me!

Epilogue

You will show me the way of life, granting
me the joy of your presence and the
pleasures of living with you forever.
—Psalm 16:11 (NLT)

Grateful Praise, Hallelujah

Jehovah God,
the Holy One,
my Lord in heaven
and here on earth,
Your majesty and power
are shining through Ya.

Your light, Your presence
fill my soul,
Your love and Spirit
Oh, so bold.
Behold Your beauty,
singing hallelujah.

Hallelujah, hallelujah,
hallelujah, hallelujah.

I praise You, Lord.
Your blessings sweet,
Your gifts of love
come silently,
as gently as
the morning, sunrise.

I seek Your face,
my daily quest,
to mend my heart
and brokenness.
I raise my hands
and pray a hallelujah.

Hallelujah, hallelujah,
hallelujah, hallelujah.

My heart is humble.
Hear me, Lord,
and save me from
my wicked ways.
You stand by me,
and I keep turning to Ya.

Your faithfulness
and steadfast love
sweep over me
from up above.
You hear my prayer.
I'm shouting hallelujah.

Hallelujah, hallelujah,
hallelujah, hallelujah.

I love You, Lord,
With all my heart.
Now, lead me where
I'll do my part
To take Your light
Into our darkened world.

I'll serve You, Lord,
Our one true way,
And love my neighbor
As You say,
To shine Your light
And sing your hallelujah.

Hallelujah, hallelujah,
hallelujah, hallelujah.

Note: This poem can be sung to the music "Hallelujah," words and music by Leonard Cohen.

References and Source Acknowledgments

Menachem Begin: Menachem Begin Quotes. BrainyQuote.com, Xplore Inc., 2017. https://www.brainyquote.com/quotes/menachembegin_720161 (accessed December 3, 2017).

Pierre Teilhard de Chardin: Pierre Teilhard de Chardin Quotes. BrainyQuote.com, Xplore Inc., 2017. https://www.brainyquote.com/quotes/pierre_teilhard_de_chardin_160888 (accessed December 11, 2017).

John Keats: John Keats Quotes. BrainyQuote.com, Xplore Inc., 2017. https://www.brainyquote.com/quotes/john_keats_138823 (accessed December 3, 2017).

Francois Mauriac: Francois Mauriac Quotes. http://www.beliefnet.com/quotes/inspiration/f/francois-muriac/no-love-no-friendship-can-cross-the-path-of-our-d.aspx (accessed December 3, 1917).

Henry David Thoreau: Henry David Thoreau Quotes. BrainyQuote.com, Xplore Inc., 2017. https://www.brainyquote.com/quotes/henry_david_thoreau_153926 (accessed December 3, 2017).

Paul Tillich: Paul Tillich Quotes. BrainyQuote.com, Xplore Inc., 2017. https://www.brainyquote.com/quotes/paul_tillich_386211 (accessed December 3, 2017).

Saint Patrick: "The Deer's Cry/Lorica/The Breastplate of St. Patrick." wowzone.com/lorica.htm (accessed December 3, 2017).

About the Author

Ray grew up in northeastern Pennsylvania, in Small Town, USA. Shortly after graduating high school, he enlisted in the US Air Force, where he spent the next seven years. He received an honorable discharge and immediately enrolled in college, receiving a BS in education with a concentration in life sciences. After moving to Connecticut, he taught junior high school life sciences, and during that time he received his MS in science education. After twelve years of public school teaching, he changed career paths and went to work for a large electric utility as a training instructor in their nuclear training division. Later, he became the curriculum development coordinator for the technical training programs and was also the accreditation coordinator for these training programs.

Over the years, Ray also pursued his personal interests in the arts, including poetry. Spontaneously and unexpectedly, one day, he woke up and started writing poetry. Ray doesn't have a formal background in the literary arts, so it has been a continuous learn-by-doing process for him over the last twenty-five years, culminating in this manuscript.

Ray lives in Connecticut with his wife, Sally, and their dog, Milo.